TENOR SAX
Showstoppers

Design: Jeannette Aquino, Frank Milone
Editor: Carol Cuellar

CONTENTS

CONTENTS

COLUMBIA PICTURES Presents RACHEL WARD, JEFF BRIDGES and JAMES WOODS
In A TAYLOR HACKFORD Film "AGAINST ALL ODDS"

AGAINST ALL ODDS
(Take a Look At Me Now)

By
PHIL COLLINS

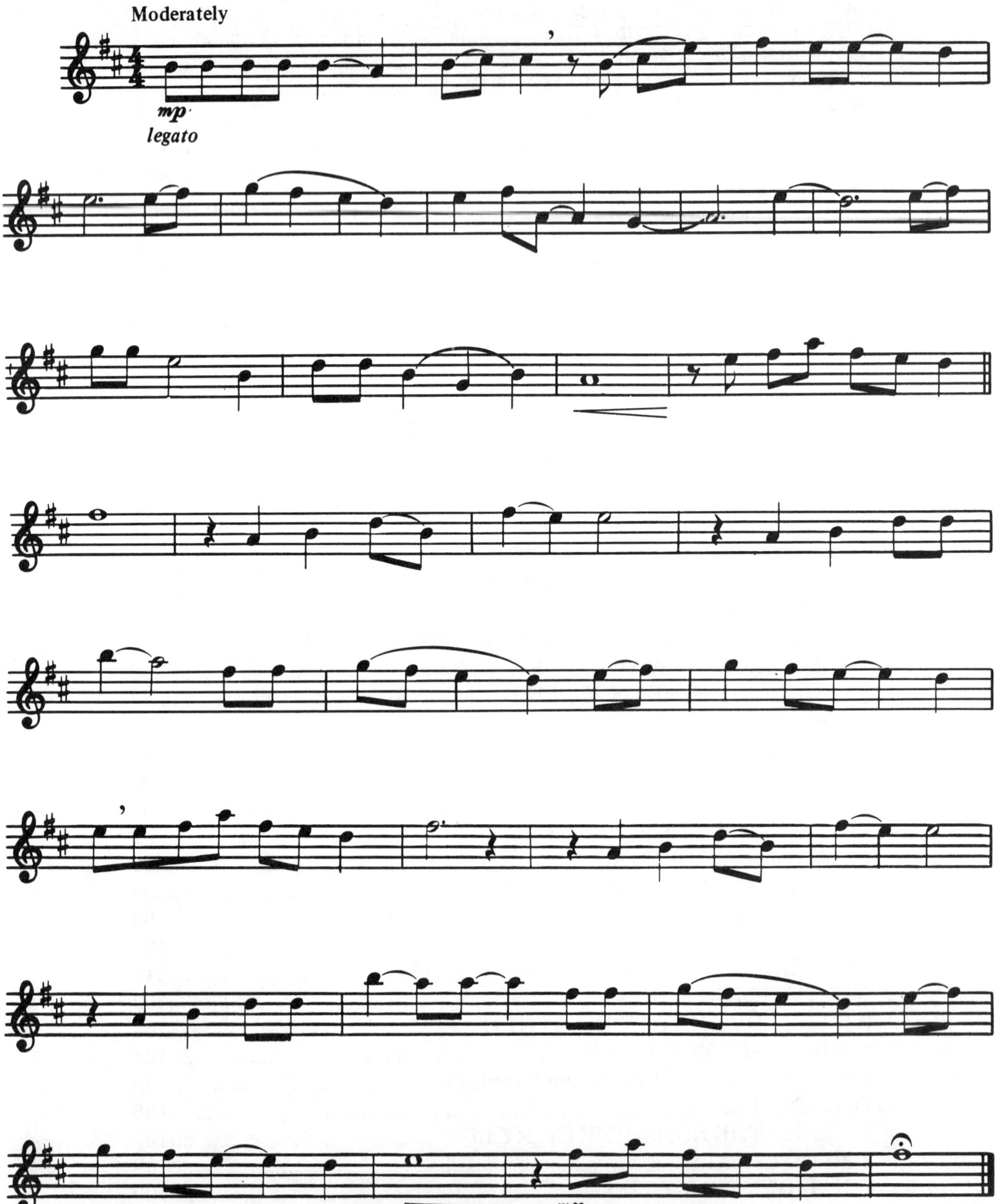

BOTH SIDES OF THE STORY

Moderate rock

legato

By PHIL COLLINS

ALWAYS

Written by
JONATHAN LEWIS, DAVID LEWIS
and WAYNE LEWIS

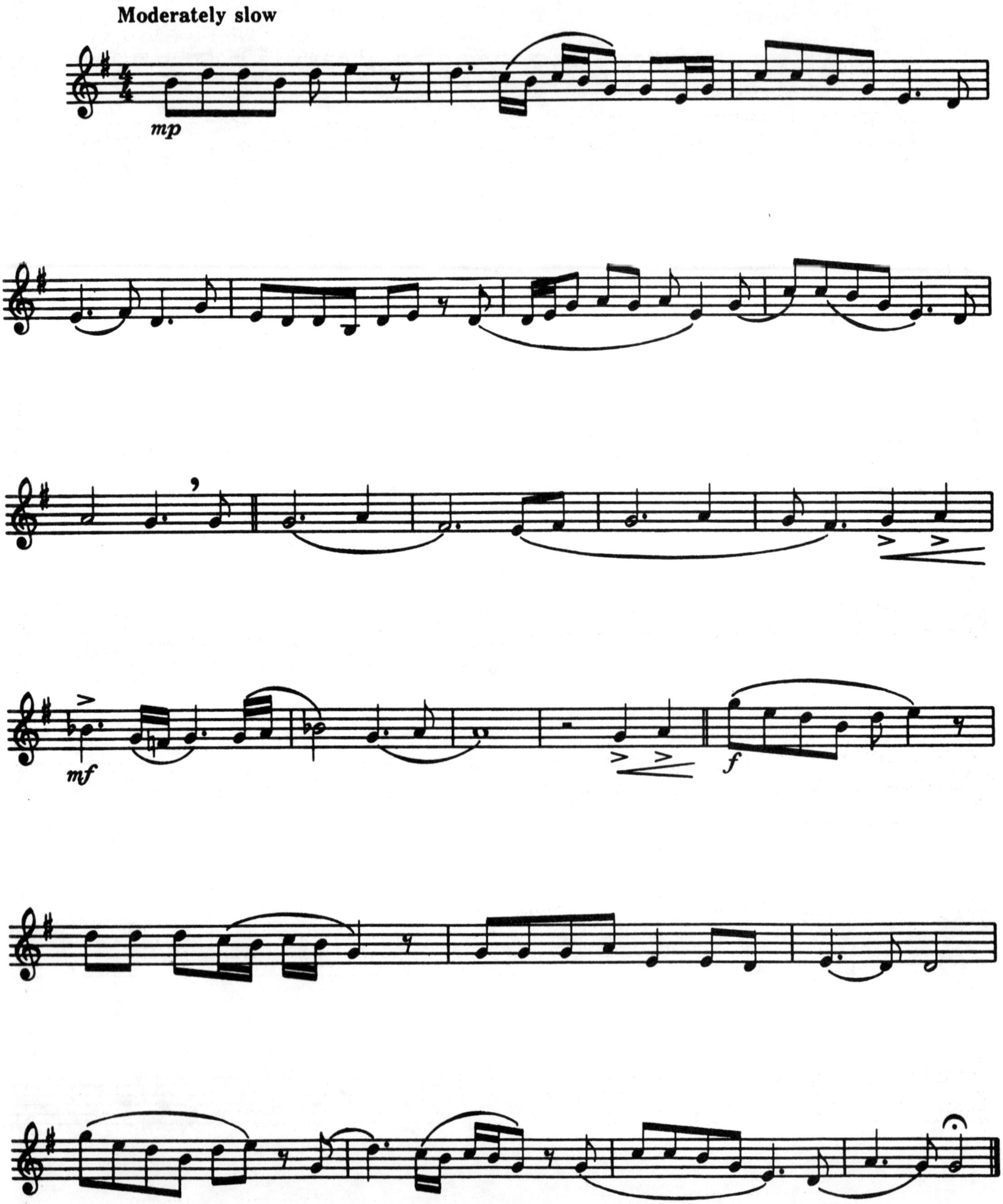

From the Motion Picture Soundtrack from Paramount Pictures' "BOOMERANG"

END OF THE ROAD

Words and Music by
BABYFACE, L.A. REID, DARYL SIMMONS

ALWAYS AND FOREVER

Words and Music by
ROD TEMPERTON

1.
2.

ANYTHING FOR YOU

Words and Music by
GLORIA M. ESTEFAN

THE DAY I FALL IN LOVE

(Love Theme from "Beethoven's 2nd")

Words and Music by CAROLE BAYER SAGER, CLIF MAGNESS and JAMES INGRAM

Moderately slow

legato

BABY, COME TO ME

By ROD TEMPERTON

Moderately

GAMES PEOPLE PLAY

Words and Music by
JOE SOUTH

CALIFORNIA GIRLS

By BRIAN WILSON

CLASSICAL GAS

By MASON WILLIAMS

From The Tri-Star Pictures film "CHANCES ARE"

AFTER ALL

(Love Theme From "Chances Are")

By
DEAN PITCHFORD and
TOM SNOW

From The "BALLET FOR A GIRL IN BUCHANNON" From The Columbia L.P. "CHICAGO"®

COLOUR MY WORLD

By JAMES PANKOW

HAVE YOU EVER SEEN THE RAIN?

Written by
J.C. FOGERTY

Moderate rock

DO YOU LOVE ME

Words and Music by
BERRY GORDY

Moderately up ♩= 126

DO YOU WANT TO KNOW A SECRET?

By
JOHN LENNON and
PAUL McCARTNEY

(Sittin' On)
THE DOCK OF THE BAY

By
STEVE CROPPER and
OTIS REDDING

DON'T CRY OUT LOUD

By
PETER ALLEN and
CAROLE BAYER SAGER

DON'T FALL IN LOVE WITH A DREAMER

By
KIM CARNES and
DAVE ELLINGSON

DON'T IT MAKE MY BROWN EYES BLUE

By RICHARD LEIGH

From The Paramount Motion Picture "SCROOGED"

PUT A LITTLE LOVE IN YOUR HEART

Words and Music by
JIMMY HOLIDAY, RANDY MYERS
and JACKIE DE SHANNON

Moderately

I CAN SEE CLEARLY NOW

Words and Music by
JOHNNY NASH

Moderate rock

FALLING IN LOVE
(Uh-Oh)

By
LAWRENCE DERMER, JOE GALDO
and RAFAEL VIGIL

Moderately

From The M-G-M Motion Picture "FAME"

FAME

Lyrics by
DEAN PITCHFORD

Music by
MICHAEL GORE

Moderately

FOR ONCE IN MY LIFE

Lyric by
RONALD MILLER

Music by
ORLANDO MURDEN

Paramount Pictures Presents A Daniel Melnick Production A Herbert Ross Film "FOOTLOOSE"

FOOTLOOSE

Written by
KENNY LOGGINS and
DEAN PITCHFORD

Fast rock and roll

To Coda
1.
2.
D.S. al Coda
Coda
poco rit.

FOR YOUR EYES ONLY

Lyrics by MICHAEL LEESON
Music by BILL CONTI

Moderately Slow

FROM A DISTANCE

Lyrics and Music by
JULIE GOLD

COLUMBIA PICTURES Presents An IVAN REITMAN Film
A BLACK RHINO/BERNIE BRILLSTEIN Production "GHOSTBUSTERS"

GHOSTBUSTERS

Words and Music by
RAY PARKER, JR.

Moderately bright rock

GIVING YOU THE BEST THAT I GOT

Words and Music by
ANITA BAKER, SKIP SCARBOROUGH
and RANDY HOLLAND

Medium ♩=108

THEME FROM "ROCKY"
(Gonna Fly Now)

By
BILL CONTI, AYN ROBBINS
and CAROL CONNORS

(From the Columbia Motion Picture "THE GREATEST") A Columbia/EMI Presentation

THE GREATEST LOVE OF ALL

Slowly

Music by MICHAEL MASSER

From the Universal Motion Picture "THE STING"

THE ENTERTAINER

By
SCOTT JOPLIN

mp
mf
mp
mf
mp
mf
mp
mf

I SWEAR

Words and Music by
GARY BAKER and FRANK MYERS

Moderately

HEY, GOOD LOOKIN'

By HANK WILLIAMS

Moderate country swing

HEY! BABY!

Words and Music by
MARGARET COBB and
BRUCE CHANNEL

HOW CAN I EASE THE PAIN

By
NARADA MICHAEL WALDEN
& LISA FISCHER

THE HOUSE OF THE RISING SUN

By
ALAN PRICE

Slow rock

HOW WILL I KNOW

Words and Music by
GEORGE MERRILL, SHANNON RUBICAM
and NARADA MICHAEL WALDEN

Moderately

From The Vestron Motion Picture "Dirty Dancing"

HUNGRY EYES

Words and Music by
FRANKE PREVITE and
JOHN DeNICOLA

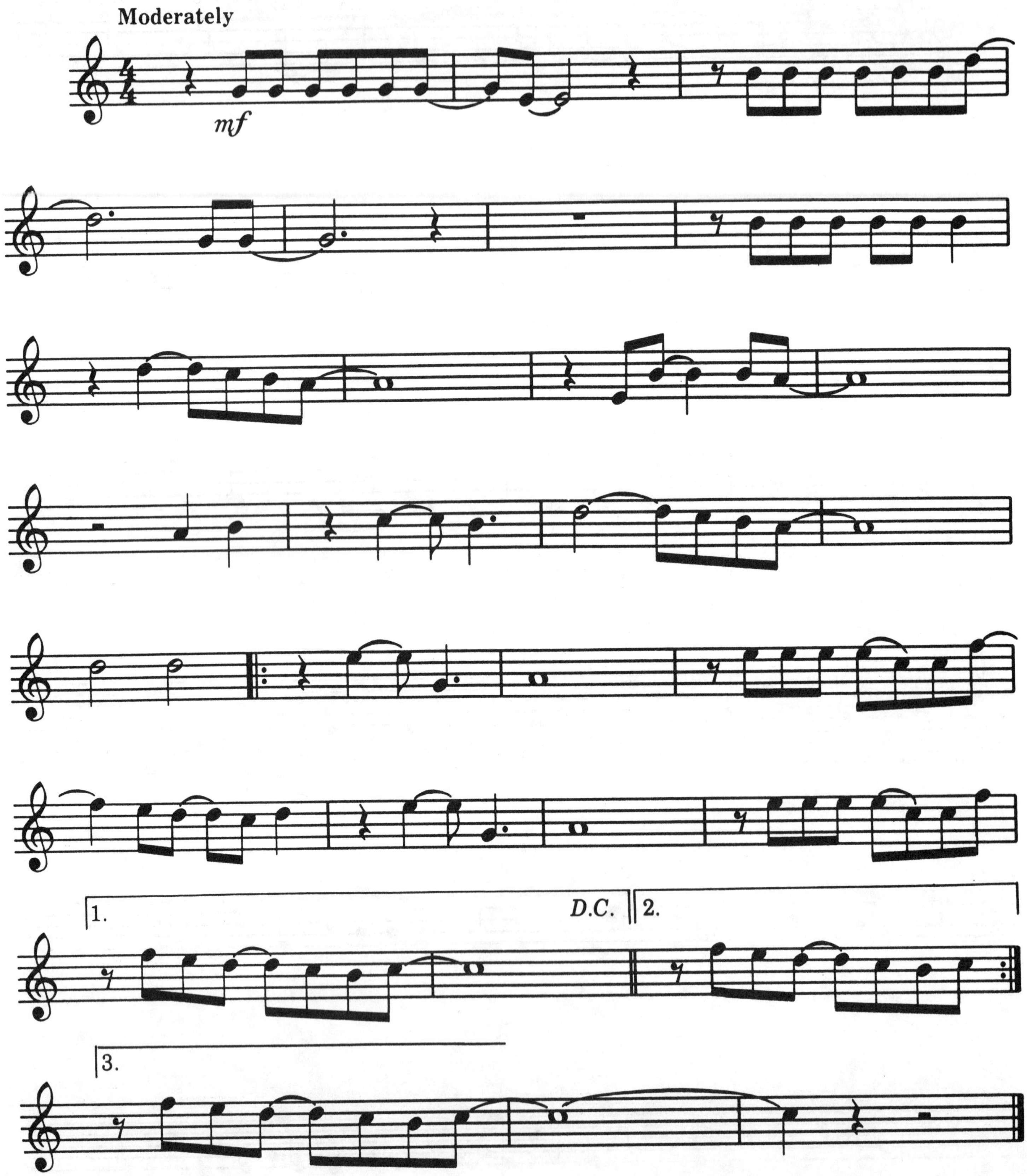

I JUST CALLED TO SAY I LOVE YOU

Words and Music by
STEVIE WONDER

('Til) I KISSED YOU

Words and Music by
DON EVERLY

(EVERYTHING I DO) I DO IT FOR YOU

By
BRYAN ADAMS, R.J. LANGE
and M. KAMEN

IF EVER YOU'RE IN MY ARMS AGAIN

Words and Music by
MICHAEL MASSER, TOM SNOW
and CYNTHIA WEIL

ISN'T SHE LOVELY

Moderately

By STEVIE WONDER

COLUMBIA PICTURES Presents a MIRAGE/PUNCH Production a Sidney Pollack Film "TOOTSIE"

IT MIGHT BE YOU
(Theme From Tootsie)

Words by
ALAN and MARILYN BERGMAN
Music by DAVE GRUSIN

Slowly, with expression

mp
f
mf
D.S. al Coda
mp
Coda
rit. e dim.
p

I'LL NEVER LOVE THIS WAY AGAIN

Words by
WILL JENNINGS

Music by
RICHARD KERR

Moderate Ballad

JUST THE TWO OF US

By
RALPH MacDONALD, WILLIAM SALTER
and BILL WITHERS

Easily

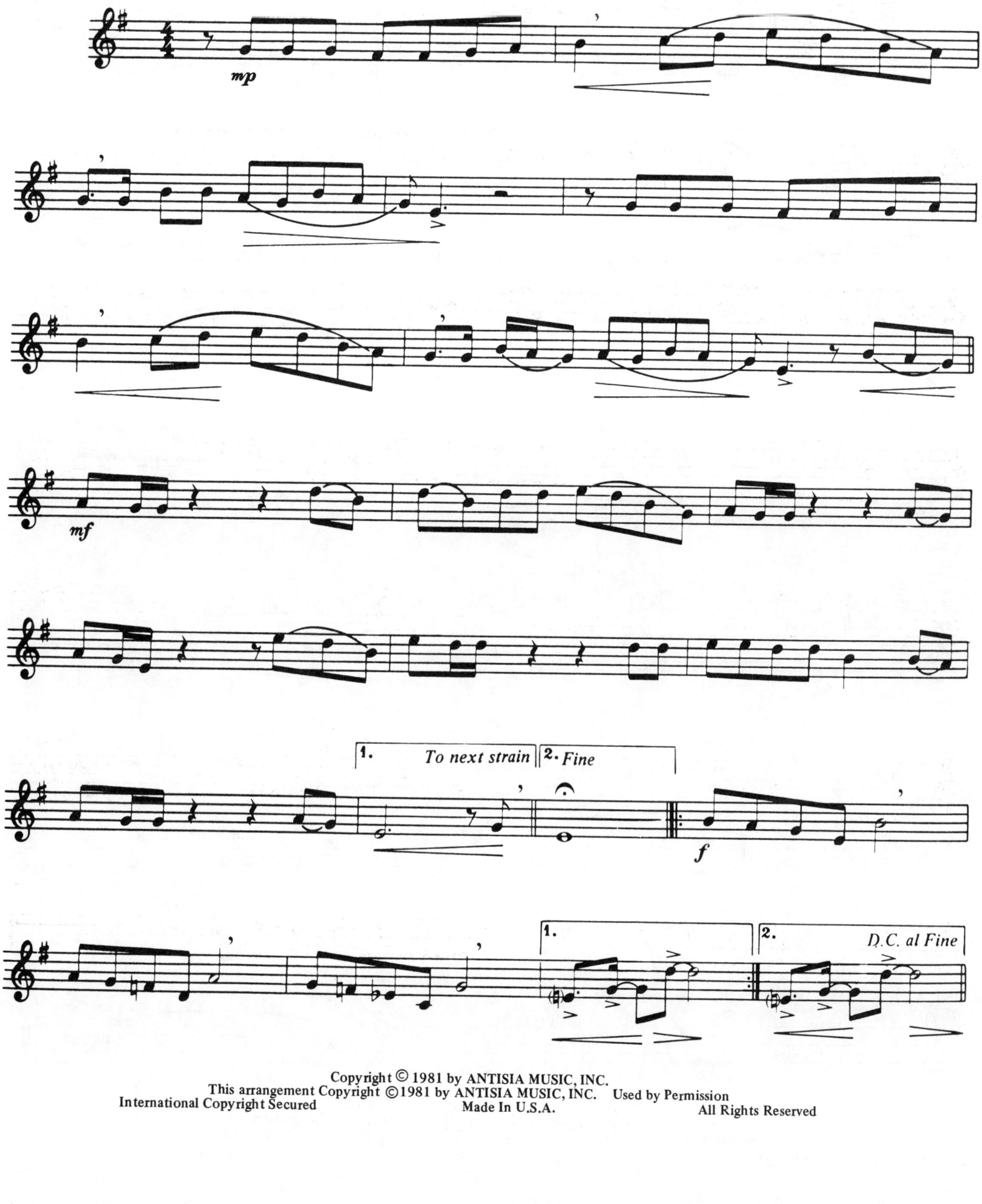

THE LADY IN RED

By
CHRIS DeBURGH

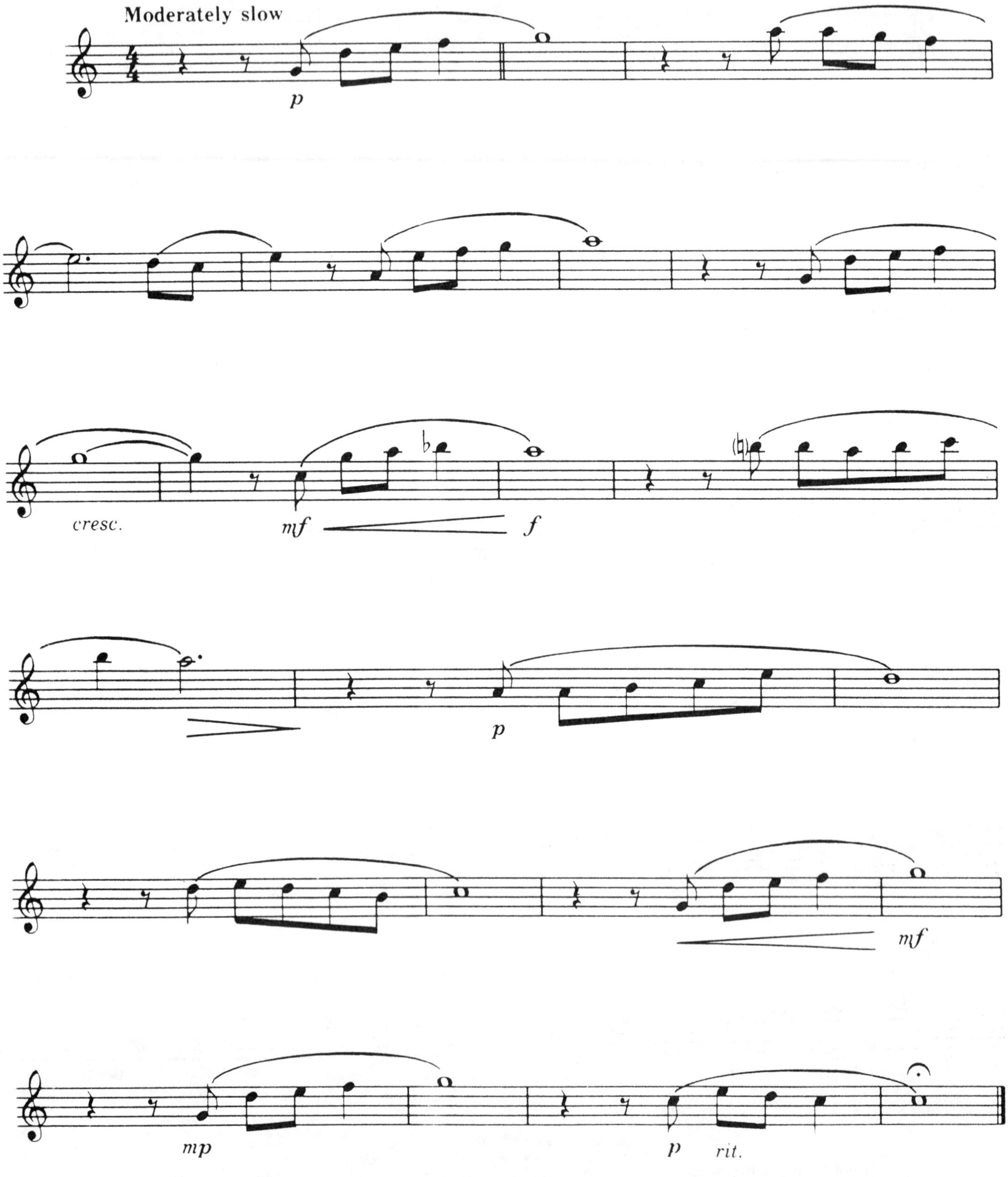

LAST DATE
(Instrumental)

By FLOYD CRAMER

Slow country swing

LINUS & LUCY

By
VINCE GUARALDI

Columbia Pictures Presents A Channel-Lauren Shuler Production
A Joel Schumacher Film "ST. ELMO'S FIRE"

LOVE THEME FROM ST. ELMO'S FIRE

(Instrumental)

By
DAVID FOSTER

Moderately Slow, with emotion

MISTY

By
JOHNNY BURKE and
ERROLL GARNER

From the Motion Picture "THREESOME"

I'LL TAKE YOU THERE

Words and Music by
ALVERTIS ISBELL

MY LOVE

Words and Music by
STEVIE WONDER

I WILL ALWAYS LOVE YOU

Words and Music by
DOLLY PARTON

From the Original Motion Picture Soundtrack 8 SECONDS

LANE'S THEME

Composed by
BILL CONTI

OH, PRETTY WOMAN

By ROY ORBISON and BILL DEES

Medium rock

ON GREEN DOLPHIN STREET

Words by NED WASHINGTON
Music by BRONISLAU KAPER

Moderately

ON THE WINGS OF LOVE

Words by JEFFREY OSBORNE
Music By PETER SCHLESS

ONE IN A MILLION YOU

By SAM DEES

From The Metro-Goldwyn-Mayer Musical Production "THE WIZARD OF OZ"

OVER THE RAINBOW

Moderately

Words by E.Y. HARBURG
Music by HAROLD ARLEN

Theme Song From The Mirisch-G&E Production, THE PINK PANTHER, A United Artists Release

THE PINK PANTHER

By HENRY MANCINI

DON'T WANNA LOSE YOU

By GLORIA ESTEFAN

Moderately slow ♩ = 80

LEAVING LAS VEGAS

Words and Music by
SHERYL CROW, BILL BOTTRELL, DAVID BAERWALD,
KEVIN GILBERT and DAVID RICKETTS

Moderate rock

MORE THAN WORDS

By
BETTENCOURT, CHERONE

RISE

By
ANDY ARMER and
RANDY BADAZZ

THE LION SLEEPS TONIGHT

(Wimoweh)

Lyrics and Revised Music by
GEORGE DAVID WEISS, HUGO PERETTI
and LUIGI CREATORE

Moderate rock

Columbia Pictures Presents A New Vision Production "WHITE NIGHTS"

SEPARATE LIVES

(Love Theme From "WHITE NIGHTS")

By
STEPHEN BISHOP

SINGING THE BLUES

By MELVIN ENDSLEY

SIR DUKE

By
STEVIE WONDER

STARDUST

Words by MITCHELL PARISH
Music by HOAGY CARMICHAEL

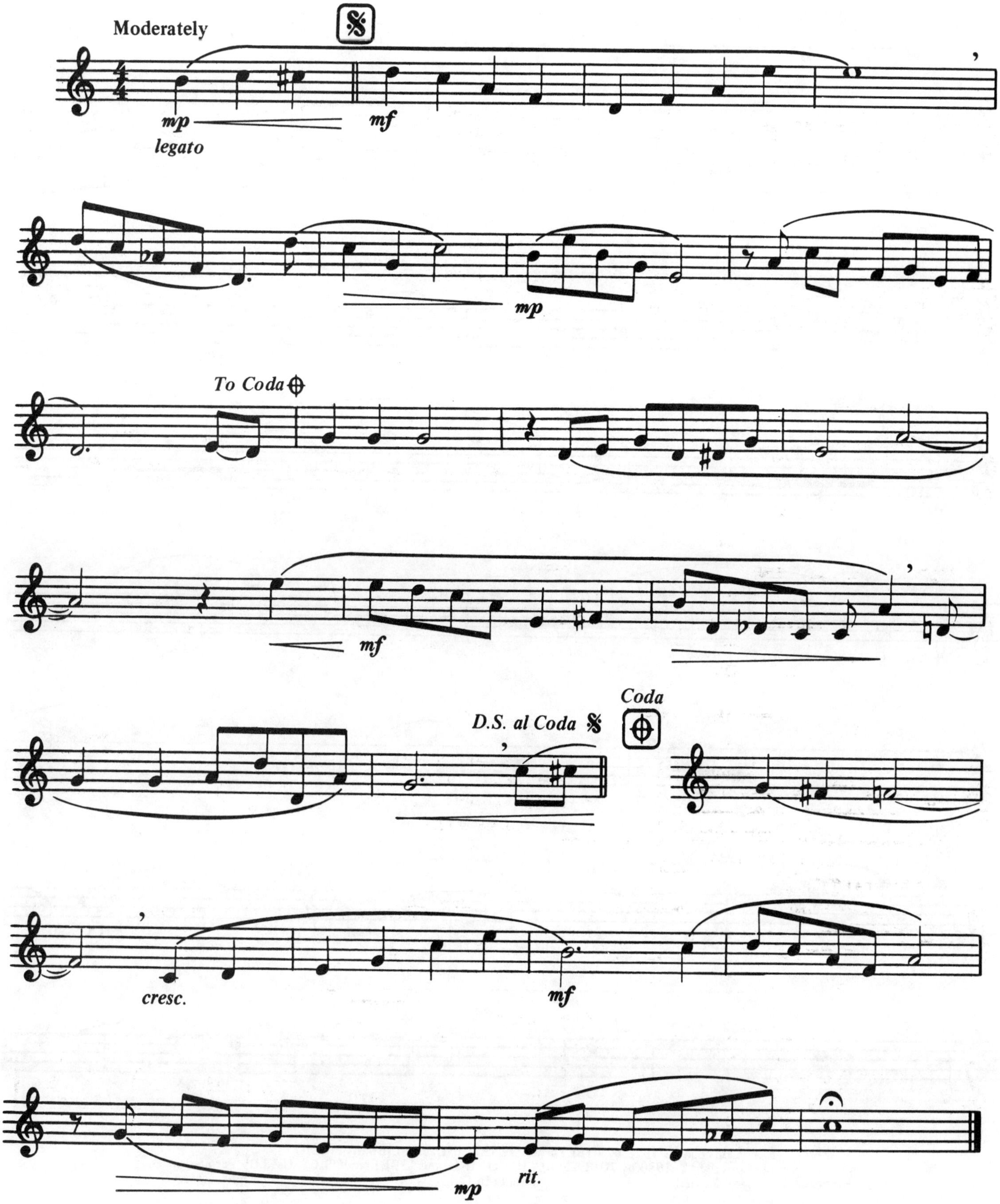

STILL

By LIONEL B. RICHIE, JR.

Columbia Pictures Presents A Channel-Lauren Shuler Production
A Joel Schumacher Film "ST. ELMO'S FIRE"

ST. ELMO'S FIRE
(MAN IN MOTION)

By
JOHN PARR and
DAVID FOSTER

Moderate Rock

SIGNS

By
LES EMMERSON

SWEET LOVE

By
ANITA BAKER, LOUIS A. JOHNSON
& GARY BIAS

LOVE SNEAKIN' UP ON YOU

Words and Music by
TOM SNOW and
JIMMY SCOTT

From the Columbia Picture "ICE CASTLES"

THEME FROM ICE CASTLES
(Through The Eyes Of Love)

Music by MARVIN HAMLISCH

Slowly, with feeling

From The United Artists Motion Picture "NEW YORK, NEW YORK"

THEME FROM NEW YORK, NEW YORK

Words by FRED EBB
Music by JOHN KANDER

Moderately, with rhythm

from the Vestron Motion Picture "Dirty Dancing"

(I'VE HAD) THE TIME OF MY LIFE

Words and Music by
FRANKE PREVITE, DONALD MARKOWITZ
and JOHN DeNICOLA

WILL YOU BE THERE

(In the Morning)

Composed by
ROBERT JOHN "MUTT" LANGE

Moderate rock

f
rit.

DON'T TURN AROUND

Words and Music by
DIANE WARREN and ALBERT HAMMOND

1.
2.
poco rit.

TRY A LITTLE TENDERNESS

By
HARRY WOODS, JIMMY CAMPBELL
and REG. CONNELLY

TO ME

Words and Music by
MACK DAVID and
MIKE REID

Slowly, with feeling

IN THIS LIFE

Words and Music by
MIKE REID and
ALLEN SHAMBLIN

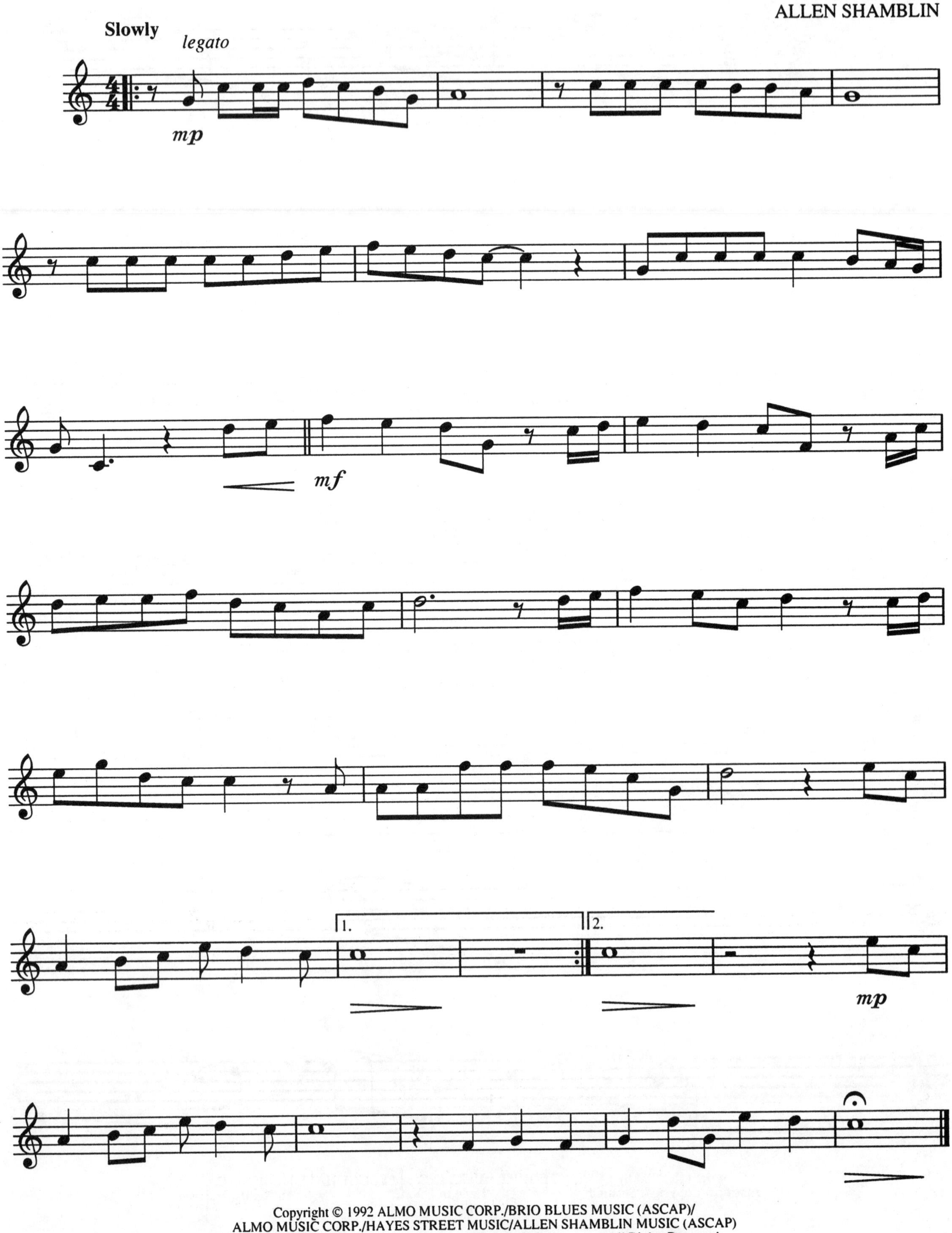

From The Broadway Musical "ANNIE"

TOMORROW

Lyric by
MARTIN CHARNIN

Music by
CHARLES STROUSE

Moderately Slow

TONIGHT I CELEBRATE MY LOVE

Words and Music by
MICHAEL MASSER and
GERRY GOFFIN

Slowly and expressively

TRAVELIN' MAN

Words and Music by
JERRY FULLER

WALKING IN MEMPHIS

By
MARC COHN

Moderately ♩ = 132

UP WHERE WE BELONG

Words by WILL JENNINGS
Music by BUFFY SAINT-MARIE
and JACK NITZSCHE

Slowly

From The Original Motion Picture Soundtrack "YENTL"

THE WAY HE MAKES ME FEEL

Lyrics by
ALAN and MARILYN BERGMAN

Music by
MICHEL LEGRAND

Slowly and expressively

WE'VE ONLY JUST BEGUN

Words by PAUL WILLIAMS
Music by ROGER NICHOLS

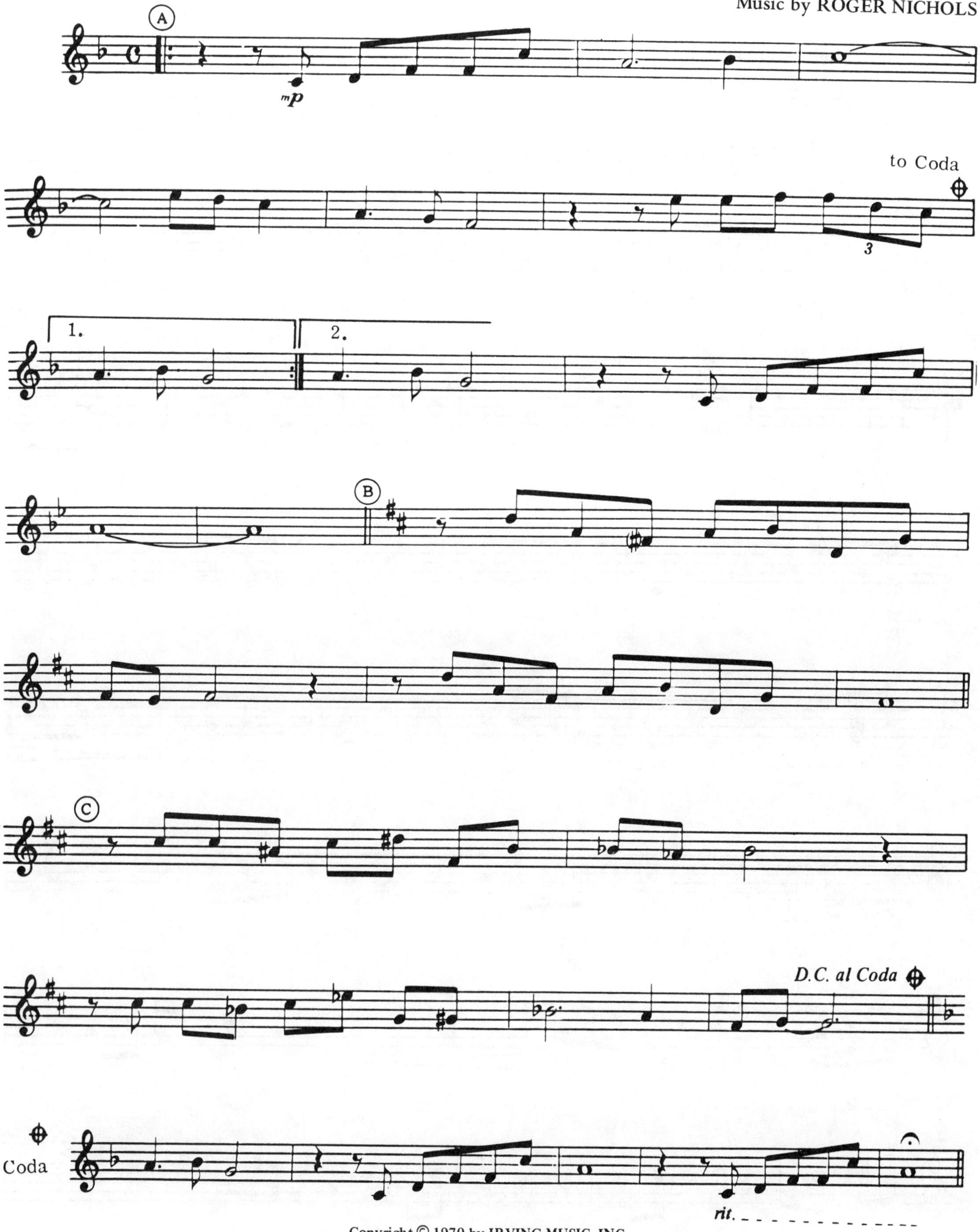

WHAT'S GOING ON

Words and Music by
ALFRED CLEVELAND, MARVIN GAYE,
RENALDO BENSON

WHAT'S LOVE GOT TO DO WITH IT

Words and Music by
GRAHAM LYLE and
TERRY BRITTEN

Moderately

A WHITE SPORT COAT
(And A Pink Carnation)

Words and Music by
MARTY ROBBINS

YOU ARE THE SUNSHINE OF MY LIFE

By
STEVIE WONDER

Moderately, with feeling

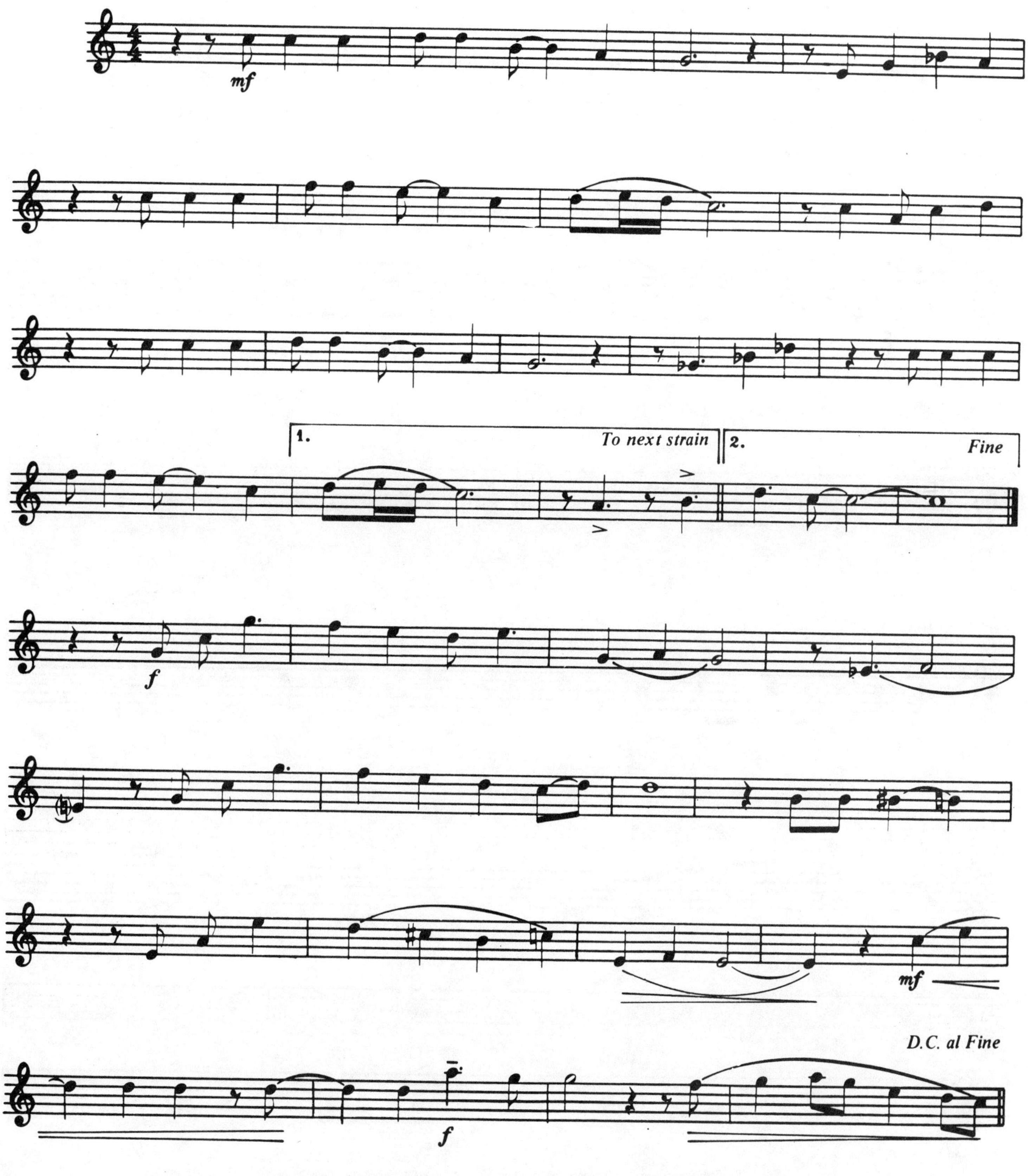

YOU AND I

By FRANK MYERS

1.
D.S.
2.

YOU GOT IT ALL

Words and Music by
RUPERT HOLMES

From the Columbia Pictures Release "YOU LIGHT UP MY LIFE"

YOU LIGHT UP MY LIFE

By
JOE BROOKS

Moderately

WHAT BECOMES OF THE BROKEN-HEARTED

Words and Music by
JAMES DEAN, PAUL RISER
and WILLIAM WEATHERSPOON

Moderately

OLD TIME ROCK & ROLL

Words and Music by
GEORGE JACKSON and
THOMAS E. JONES III

The two cells that do possess the full complement of chromatin material later turn out to be the germ cells. Thus different cells of the blastula have different chromatin content and really possess quantitative differentiation. The differential DNA quantum has differential nucleo-cytoplasmic interaction. A similar phenomenon has been noticed in some Diptera.

***Gene Amplification*:** In the formation of amphibian oocytes at certain stage in which the rRNA synthesis is very active. The gene for rRNA exists in a large number of copies. In some cases where the genome of the oocyte was tetraploid it contained not just four nucleoli but nearly 1000. Each one of these nuclei actively synthesizes rRNA. This leads to the conclusion that the oocyte contains many copies of the genes for rRNA. The diploid genome of *Xenopus laevis* contains nearly 1600 copies of the genes for rRNA and all of them are clustered in the nucleolar organizer region.

Another interesting case of gene amplification is noticed in the lampbrush chromosome of Amphibian oocytes. Here again extra copies of tRNA and mRNA molecules are met with that have a regulatory influence over the process of development.

Genetic Lesions: In 1958 researchers at Oxford University found a mutant variety of *Xenopus laevis* that possessed only one nucleolus instead of the usual two. These animals are called 1.nu.individual. This deficiency of nucleolar material does not, however, prevent normal development. When the mutants were mated (1.nu x l.nu) the offsprings were of the followings types: Normal form (2.nu), heterozygous (l.nu) and homozygous mutant (0.nu) in the typical Mendelian ratio of 1:2:1. The (0.nu) individual without any nucleolus does not develop beyond the early stages. The (0.nu) mutant is formed due to the deletion of 28S and 18S rRNA genes from one of the chromosomes.

(B) Chemical Changes of DNA

There are two methods by which DNA may be modified chemically. They are :

(a) Alkylation.

(b) Methylation.

The enzymes necessary for bringing about these reactions are already found within the cell itself. The reactions affect particular nucleotide bases of the DNA which in turn alter other results. Of these methylation takes place only after DNA replication and so this reaction has to take place every time after the DNA replication is completed.

Control of Differentiation during Transcription : At the level of transcription during the process of protein synthesis, the various genes present in the chromosomes of a developing embryo may be controlled by the following methods:

Gene Regulation by Histones : The chromosomes contain nucleoproteins. The nucleic acid part of this is made up of a DNA while the protein part is predominantly made up of a kind of proteins called histones. These histones contain mostly basic amino acids like arginine, lysine and histidine. The DNA molecule has free acidic groups of phosphoric acid on the outer surface, which are able to have firm bonds with the NH_2 groups of the basic amino acids present in the histones. Thus this association becomes intimate.

This association of DNA with histones prevents the DNA from interacting with other substances present in the cytoplasm. This view has been expressed by Stedman (1950) and Bloch (1962). The DNA is thus deprived of the opportunity of serving as templates for the production of mRNA. Experimental proof in support of the above view is available. Cell-free preparations containing DNA from calf thymus and RNA polymerase taken from *Bacillus megagaterium* synthesize RNA in presence of RNA precursors. When histones were added to this mixture RNA